HER NAME IS VIKING

The Amazing True Story
Of the Last Longship
To Cross the Atlantic

To
Everyone
Who seeks Adventure

FORWARD

In the small Illinois town of Geneva, forty miles outside of Chicago and nearly a thousand miles from the nearest ocean, a longboat lies at rest. She is the last of her kind to navigate across the North Atlantic. In 1893 she sailed alone from Norway to Chicago, crewed by 12 brave men, bent on a mission to prove that the Norse – not Columbus – were the first Europeans to find and settle the Americas.

She attracted thousands at the World's Columbian Exhibition, the Chicago World's Fair of 1893. She has sailed the Mississippi River to New Orleans. She has spent decades docked near what is now Chicago's Museum of Science and Industry, has been sheltered under a wooden structure in the city's Lincoln Park. Today, she rests in Good Templar Park, Geneva, under a canopy. The state of Illinois has listed her as one of the state's 10 most endangered landmarks. But she is protected by Friends of the Viking Ship, an organization dedicated to her preservation.

Hundreds see her every year, and learn about her construction, her adventures, and the ongoing efforts to preserve her.

Her name is *Viking*.

THE MOTHERSHIP

This is a true story of bravery, daring, and high adventure, with a smattering of betrayal and tragedy to season it. The evidence remains in our public eye, and it is attested not only by eyewitnesses, but a participant.

And it begins with a pile of dirt.

This particular pile of dirt was located in a farm in Sandar, Sandefjord, Vestfold, Norway. It was, as these things go, a large pile of dirt, about 17 feet tall and 150 feet in diameter, almost the size of a small hill, and it had a name. The locals called it Gokstadhaugen, the king's burial mound. They said that, ages ago, a pagan king had been buried there. They said that the ground was haunted. They said that under the earth, gold and jewels mighty swords had been buried.

Of course, there were many such places in Norway, and just because people said "King's burial mound" or even "gold and jewels" it did not mean much. The mound was on a farm, a working farm. And so, every year it was ploughed over, and then crops were planted, and harvested in their time. And every year, the mound grew just a little smaller.

Until the fateful year of 1890. In that winter, the teenage sons of the farm were bored. They decided that they would burrow down to the riches buried below, and have a little fun determining if the tales were true. So, they began to dig.

These boys were not children, and they were not city dwellers. They were strong teenage boys who were used to using tools and doing manual labor. Their hole went deep into the heavy, frozen Norwegian soil. They kept at their work for days, and when the hole was five feet deep, they uncovered the badly rotten bow of an ancient longboat.

Photograph from the Oslo Museum of the Viking ship, public domain

Although this was not the treasure they were seeking, it was certainly a thrilling discovery. The boys told their exciting tale over and over, and people came to see the exposed parts of the ship. By spring the news had reached all the way to Oslo, and Nicolay Nicolaysen, founder of The Society for the Preservation of Ancient Norwegian Monuments, and Norway's first nationally-funded antiquarian, came to see the dig.

He immediately realized the importance of the site, and requested that the digging stop. He proposed going into the mound from the side, so as not to destroy whatever was buried in it. The farm's owner agreed to this, and work began on a formal archaeological excavation.

The mound was in fact a burial site for, not a king, but a tall, strong man who had died in battle. Deep inside the hill was a structure built of logs and covered with birch bark. Bits of silk and gold thread indicate that the inner roof of the structure had been covered with some sort of rich hangings.

The log structure sheltered a Viking ship. Most of the boat had been buried in blue clay, and this part of the ship was remarkably preserved. The protruding bow and stern posts had been covered in normal dirt and they were badly rotted. Inside the front of the boat, archeologists found pieces of white wool cloth, sewn with red stripes, which was probably the ship's sail. Behind the mast was a burial chamber, where the deceased had been laid to rest on a bed, surrounded by the remains of twelve horses, six dogs, two hawks of a type local to the site, and a pair of peacocks.

The deceased was about 40 years old, six feet three inches tall, and had died from wounds to his legs (striking at the legs was a common tactic of Viking fighters). Though both legs were wounded, a deep gash to his left thigh was almost undoubtably what had killed him.

Contrary to the local legends, the burial held no gold or jewels, probably because looters had stolen them centuries before. Any weapons buried there had also been removed. But 64 shields, painted alternatingly yellow and black, decorated the sides of the buried ship. The deceased was also surrounded by a gaming board, kitchen tools, harness for the horses made of leather and decorated with iron and bronze, a sledge, a cart, a tent, and two smaller boats. In all the time since, we have never discovered exactly who he was. Not a king or the relative of a king. Yet definitely a warrior.

Years later, more excavation work discovered a trading village quite close to the mound. Archaeologists also determined that, because the sea was about 4 feet higher in those days, the Gokstad burial was near to the sea at the time of its construction.

Gokstad, as the ship came to be called, though it was centuries old, was one of the best-preserved Viking ships ever found, and also one of the largest. Archaeologists were able to restore her by disassembling the parts, steaming the warped wood and twisting it back into its original shape. The rotten pieces could be replaced with modern timber.

Gokstad is clinker-built, which means that she is constructed from planks which overlap each other. Each plank is individually shaped. A clinker-built vessel can be nailed together, with one nail going completely through an outside plank and into an inner board. But *Gokstad* was built using bolts and screws. In a clinker-built ship, each plank is integral to the construction of the entire ship.

The resulting ship was (and is) beautiful and graceful. She did not have a dragon head or tail, which may indicate she was

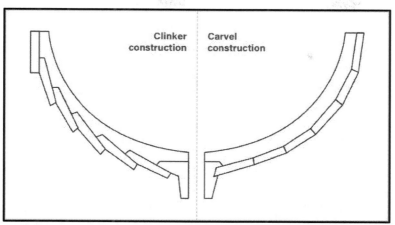

Illustration courtesy of Wikimedia Commons

a trading ship rather than a raiding ship, though no one is completely sure. She is about 73 feet long and about 17 feet wide, but only a few feet deep. This was the primary argument against the idea of a Viking longship making long sea voyages – the extremely shallow ship would be prone to taking on water from every wave.

The ship was made of tapered planks, 16 per side. The garboard planks (those on the bottom of the ship) are nearly vertical where they attach to the keel. These planks are narrow and remain only slightly wider to take the turn of the bilge (the area where the bottom of the boat turns to become the side of the boat). The planks that rise above the waterline are progressively wider. Each oak plank tapers slightly in cross section to allow it to overlap the plank above by a little more than an inch, in normal clinker (lapstrake) style. The planks are held together by iron rivets, about 7 inches apart where the planks lie straight, and about 5 inches apart where the planks turn, and has one attachment point for each plank. The inside of the stem is cut into a v shape so the ship builders could place

Gokstad, in the Museum of the Viking Ship, Norway

the connecting rivets in the side boards during construction or repair.

The ship does not have a permanent deck. Instead, each crossbeam, or rib, has a cut about one inch wide and deep. These provided a sort of ledge, holding boards that formed the deck. Storage chests on top of the temporary deck could be used as seats when rowing. Most likely, on longer voyages chests, supplies, or other heavy objects, were stored below the deck boards to act as ballast.

The ship was built to carry thirty-two rowers, and the upper planks have hole in them that allowed the oars to come through. When the ship was using only the sail, small square hatches covered the holes to keep them watertight.

The square sail, made of red and white striped wool, was about 1,200 square feet in area. This, it is estimated, would have given the ship a top speed of 12 knots (14 mph), a very respectable speed for a wind-powered vessel. The builder had hinged the forty-three-foot mast at the base, so it could be raised and lowered.

The design of the steering mechanism was different from other ships in use when she was discovered. Instead of a rudder directly in the rear of the boat, the *Gokstad* had a block of wood attached to her right (starboard) rear, using tree roots instead of iron bolts. The block was called a *wart* and its purpose was to hold a single long oar, which was used for steering. While the ship was traveling in shallow water, this rudder could be raised very quickly so it did not touch the bottom. It is easy to imagine that the basic design of these ships was inspired by the needs of raiders. These men would have wanted to sail close to the coastline, in shallow water, and possibly travel up rivers which might not be very deep. They wanted to move quickly. And, if they needed to, they also wanted to be able to make a quick getaway. Because the front and the back of the ship were shaped much the same, the crew only needed to turn around on their benches and row the opposite direction to get their ship traveling in reverse.

The antiquarians immediately realized that the *Gokstad* was very old, and in modern times, an analysis of the growth rings of the trees used to build her suggests that she was made of trees that were felled around 890 AD. This was the height of Norse expansion.

Modern boat-building tends to favor carvel construction, in which the keel of the ship is the vessel's backbone, and ribs reaching outward from the keel give shape to the vessel, while the boards forming the ship's skin are primarily there to keep the water out. The advantage that carvel has over clinker is that it can be made using any quality of wood. Carval boats are also usually made with sawn timber. Saws are difficult to make, and they cut against the grain of the wood, which does not take best advantage of the wood's strength.

On a clinker-built boat, only very select wood will do. Much like a human skeleton, in a clinker-built boat, the frame – which is built inside the clinker "skin," is there primarily to transmit force for movement. It doesn't have to hold the boat together. These boats are designed to be flexible – move with the water instead of fighting against it. "Sea-serpent" is a metaphor the Vikings used to describe their ships.

The Vikings built their boats using simple tools. You can make a Viking boat with nothing but an axe – but they used them in sophisticated ways. They followed the grain of the wood, to get the most strength and flexibility for the lowest weight.

The details of how the wood was shaped to form the contours of the boat is very intricate. Modern engineers have used complex computer analysis to help them understand the details of how the individual pieces were melded into a whole. This is not to say that the people of 1000 years ago had some kind of supernatural knowledge or tools. They simple understood their materials in a very intimate way. I like to think that building a Viking ship was like making a piece of clothing. The pieces are all designed to move as they fit together, with no one part being more important that any of the others.

Another detail about the ships built by the ancient Norse is that they used wet, uncured wood. This way, as the sap dried from the wood, it set itself into the desired shape. Viking ship builders also practiced the art of training young saplings to grow into shapes that would be useful to ship builders. If they knew they would need a curved plank, they would train a tree to grow with the proper bend.

Shipwrights also took the natural features of growing trees into account. For example, if they wanted to add an oar-hole to a plank, the best place to do this was at a place where the tree had grown a branch, this part of the wood being stronger.

This is hardly ever practiced in modern times, as it might take most of the lifetime of a tree to create a specifically formed piece of wood. And given the extremely long lifespan of an oak tree, - perhaps 50 years to reach full maturity - young boys must have grown up besides the trees that they would later use in ship building. Perhaps their fathers took them on walks through the forest, pausing to show their sons how a young oak was coming along, and speaking of the years ahead, when the boy would be a man, and he, or perhaps even his sons after him, could use the shaped tree to build an exceptional ship.

THE WORLD'S FAIR

Everyone was talking about the International Exhibition in 1893. So-called "World's Fairs" were a fairly new phenomena, a place where many nations could, temporarily, meet in peace to compare technological advances and celebrate their culture and art.

This fair would be the first of its kind to take place in the young United States, and American cities had competed fiercely for the honor of hosting it. When Chicago finally won out over New York, the Chicago planners vowed to create an Exposition the likes of which the world had never seen before.

They were facing steep competition. Paris's The Exposition Universelle de 1889 had featured displays by 35 countries, produced the Eiffel Tower, and hosted over seventeen million guests. Chicago planned to have 46 attending countries, and the city's greatest architects worked on building designs and landscaping they hoped would deeply impress the world.

Norway was contributing displays important for both groundbreaking technology and historic and cultural importance. They intended to demonstration innovations in insulation, display works of prominent Norwegian women artists, and show the ancient culture of the country by erecting an example of a historic Norse "Stave Church." This impressive building reproduced a type of edifice in use for 1000 years, and yet innovated by a modern Norwegian builder who had created a traditional building that could be disassembled for shipment and then re-assembled in record time.

The Norwegian people also wanted to show off the recently uncovered *Gokstad*. It was such a recent discovery, and one which inspired great pride in the accomplishments of the ancient Norse people.

Even more important, the 1893 fair intended to celebrate Christopher Columbus's "discovery" of the New World in 1492. For years, American children had been taught about this "discovery" in spite of strong evidence that the first European to set foot on North America was almost certainly Leif Ericson, a Norseman, some 500 years before Columbus set sail.

Columbus, however, fulfilled the requirements of the "Great Man" teaching theory, which was in fashion at the time. This teaching concept held that the best, most inspiring method of teaching history was to present it through the series of lives and accomplishments of "Great Men." This, educators believed, would inspire children to attempt great accomplishments of their own. Columbus had been a white Christian male, who had conceived a novel idea, maintained it through much derision and hardship, gotten funding from Christian monarchs, and performed his explorations more-or-less alone. (The efforts of the uneducated sailors who actually operated the boats were not considered.)

In fact, even the central idea behind Columbus's explorations has been misconstrued. His voyages were based, not on the fact that the world was round, but on a miscalculation of its size. The ancient Greeks had performed experiments long before the birth of Christ that proved a round earth, and gave a close approximation of its size – about 39,250 miles, which is an error of only 2%. Columbus had miscalculated, and come up with an estimate of only 21,600 miles, or an error of about 25%. Through his mistake, he believed that India and China were only a few weeks sailing, if one headed due west.

Leif Ericson, who was not a Christian (a very important fact to 19th century Americans), did not seem to have any grand ideas. He possessed a technologically advanced boat and a desire to see where it could take him. He sailed from Greenland to what is now Canada in 999 and founded a settlement there. Norwegians were quite familiar with this fact, and American scholars knew about the Norse sagas describing the event. But they were fond of Columbus.

Someone – possibly a military officer - decided that the best way to impress Americans was to make a Viking ship, exactly like the ones which had sailed the seas a millennia ago, and sail her across the Atlantic, through the Erie Canal, through the Great Lakes, to the Chicago Fair. With the discovery of the *Gokstad* they had to very good model to work from.

Christen Christensen agreed to build the replica in his shipyard, the Deserve shipyard in Sandefjord, Norway. Interested people formed a committee. The venture was crowd-funded, in the style of the day. Newspapers and magazine advertisements requested funds, and individual people sent cash or checks by mail to the committee.

Christensen was a very well-respected man (he would be knighted in 1895) and famous for his good business sense and ability to innovate ancient companies with new technologies. He also had a reputation for daring-do. Only a few years before, he had attempted, with another man, to sail a twenty-foot-long open boat, the *Ocean,* from Norway to Canada. While that attempt had failed, he was intensely interested in trying again, this time with a truly remarkable ship.

The challenge of recreating a thousand-year-old ship was something that had never been tried before. Many of the materials could no longer be found in Norway and needed to be outsourced. In addition, having a finished boat was not the same as having instructions on how to build that boat. The techniques of building longships had been lost long ago.

Nevertheless, the shipyard did their best. Unfortunately for us, however, they worked in total secrecy, leaving us nothing in the way of descriptions or photos of the progress.

They were faithful to the original, even reproduced features of the *Gokstad* that they did not understand or think would work. The steering mechanism was a matter of special concern. No one thought that the arrangement of an oar on the side of the ship would be nearly effective enough to keep the ship going in the right direction. Still, the wart, strengthened rib and steering oar were faithfully produced. Even the detail of attaching the lowermost strakes with spruce roots was followed.

They named her *Viking*.

When speaking of boats, when a replica is made of a historic vessel and is intended to reproduce her as accurately as possible, the new ship is said to be the daughter of the original vessel. And so, *Viking* is the daughter of *Gokstad*.

The shipyard provided the brand-new *Viking* with a back-up steering mechanism that could be bolted into place while at sea. In addition, they stocked the longboat with the latest in mechanical pumps, in case seawater came in over the low sides, the latest in zinc storage boxes for food and supplies, and a fancy one-of-a-kind chart holder.

The trip was going to be a dangerous one. Anything lost at sea would be nearly impossible to replace, and so a special box was designed to hold the maps (sea charts). This included a glass panel on the top, with the map as a scroll, moveable by outside cranks, so that the precious directions would never have to be at the mercy of wind and water.

Details related to Viking culture were also included. A beautifully carved "chieftain's seat" as included at the rear of the boat, and the deck boards included marked circles to define where each of the rowers would stand to defend the ship if she were attacked. Of course, no one expected to actually need to defend the ship, but the sailor appreciated these details.

Safety concerns were met by providing the ship with a small boat, carried crosswise in the stern of the ship, and the latest in emergency floatation devices, a very large piece of cork, big enough for the whole crew to crawl onto in an emergency.

It is difficult for people today to understand how very dangerous this journey would be. The sailors who manned the *Viking* did not have any idea how she would perform on the journey. Yet their lives would depend on her. The ship did not carry a radio to signal for help. They had no modern life preservers – only pillows stuffed with reindeer hair, which acted as floatation devices. GPS did not exist; they would calculate their position by the sun and stars. Food and water would be in good supply – the sailors remarked that they could have lived on it for a year, but storage was primitive, without refrigeration. Cooking could only be done in a kind of metal stove near the mast – a dangerous thing on a wooden boat. The only shelter the boat offered was a tent that could be pitched in the middle. Once at sea, they would be almost entirely on their own, powered only by wind and oars.

Crew of the *Viking* – Note the clothing, which was not costumes, but the common working garb of Norwegian sailors at the time.

Ship captain Magnus Andersen, who had been the captain on Christen Christensen's previous expedition, was chosen to head the journey, and the crew selected to man the ship had the highest regard for him and the utmost faith.

Andersen had been a seaman at fifteen, become a first mate by nineteen, and was a captain by twenty-two. While the *Ocean* expedition was not successful, he had made a name for himself. Indeed, when a rumor went around that Captain Anderson would not be leading them after all, the sailors declared that they would not sail under any other leader.

First mate was Johan Gustav Gundersen. He was forty-three years old. He had left home at 14, and had worked as a captain and first mate. He had also endured a shipwreck below the equator as captain of the *Winnipeg,* while his wife and two children were aboard. Everyone was able to get into lifeboats, and after three days, they reached a European colony and safety.

Second mate was Christen Christensen, whose sailing experience may not have suggested a higher title, but whose financial support rated an officer's position. He had gone to sea at 14, a common life choice for Norwegian boys. Many of them spent a year or two as sailors milestone in their lives.

Jens Bing was the youngest of the crew, only 20. He also had gone to sea very young.

Johan Eriksen was thirty. He had been a non-commissioned officer in the Norwegian Navy, and had sailed to both the Arctic and the Americas.

Fredrik Oscar Frantzen was forty, and had been at sea so long he had almost lost count of the years. His specialty was navigation, but his job aboard the Viking would be Steward, or cook.

Lars Løkke was twenty-two years old. He had started his sailing career at the comparatively late age of 17, but had already served as mate on several voyages, and had gone as far as America.

Johannes Brun Moeller was twenty-five. He had satisfied his longing for travel by sailing to several foreign countries before settling down in his father's fish shop.

Bent Nygaard was thirty-nine, and had sailed for nine years as a mate and a captain. He was selected as the Viking's carpenter – an important job on a wooden ship.

Severin Martinius Simonsen was twenty-eight. Like so many of the others, he went to sea immediately after his religious confirmation at fourteen. He had spent four years living in San Francisco.

Oscar Solberg was thirty-seven, and a world traveler who had often voyaged to Australia and New Guinea.

Rusmus Elias Rasmussen had been selected as the ship's bosun, in charge of her sails, her work schedules, and her equipment. He was thirty-nine, a lay preacher on the boats he had crewed, and had sailed all over the world.

They were an adventurous bunch, men who had done much and had not made a fuss about any of it. To a man, they were familiar with the hardships of the sea, and expected no more than a tough trip, with perhaps a moment of glory at the end. What they got was much more, in many ways.

Rasmussen, who went often by his initials, R.E., was enough of a scholar that his friends persuaded him to write an account of the voyage. He did so, and the book – *Viking, from Norway to America* – can still be found in both the original Norwegian and in English translation, and it is well worth the trouble to find and read it.

Rasmussen's only fault was that he took so much for granted in his story of the sea. What did the men eat? He did not trouble to write it down. He lists ingredients, but not how they were used: flour, sugar, prunes, raisins, coffee, and rice. We do know that the men were very grateful for fresh fish in the middle of the journey. What were the details of their daily work? Probably much like that of any other ship, Rasmussen does not bother to fill in the details. We know that the crew was divided into "watches" or work crews. Sometimes these are referred to as "port and starboard" crews, other times as "fore and aft" crews. The basic meaning of this was that there were two work crews, and they alternated work times so that no one was always stuck with an undesirable schedule.

Rasmussen's job as bosun was largely to make the boat "go" – to trim the sails in such a way that they offered the maximum "draw" or driving force. He immediately used the fairly crude tools available to the ancient Norse to set up a contemporary sail plan: a triangular sail in the very front, between the mast and the bow, reefs in the mainsail that would allow precise control over how much fabric was exposed to the wind.

Was this true to the ancient ship's original sailors? We don't know. But Rasmussen had the care of his own crew under his responsibility, and it was his duty to see that they were safe. This meant a complete use of all his knowledge.

This whole expedition, by the way, is one of the earliest examples of *experimental archaeology*. This is a situation when archaeologists give artifacts to the sort of people who might actually use them. A tool they suspect might have been useful to leather worker is handed to a leather worker. A Jewish artifact is given for analysis to a Jewish family. Often ancient tools are nearly identical to the same as tools in use 3,000 years later. In 1893, a thousand-year-old ship was given into the hands of sailors.

ACROSS THE NORTH SEA

Before she set sail, Viking was displayed at Kristiania, where she was visited by Norway's Crown Prince and members of Norway's Parliament. Ticket-buying visitors were also allowed on board. It was now that *Viking*'s crew began to appreciate her. Rasmussen, a cautious man, was eager to see how she held up under the weight of so many sight-seers, and was amazed to realize that, fully loaded, she rode only 3 inches lower in the water.

Already the crew of other ships were expressing doubts that the *Viking* could make it all the way to Chicago.

From Kristiania, *Viking* sailed to Bergen, her official place of departure. Nine thousand tickets were sold to climb aboard her, and the crew enjoyed invitations to nightly parties in their honor.

Before sailing, the ship was unloaded, given a general inspection, cleaned, and oiled. Then everything was carefully reloaded, and tied down. In addition to her Viking-style small boat, she was given a modern boat. Both were put away in the stern.

Sunday, April 29, 1893, *Viking* set sail from Bergen. Since she did not have any kind of motor, she was towed into the sea-lanes by a tugboat named (appropriately) the *Leif Erikson*. A few important guests rode along on the beginning of her journey, and dozens of boats sailed alongside.

Viking was decked out in her best. Although the *Gokstad* had not had a dragon head or tail, V*iking* was supplied with both. Providing them was a matter of national pride. The bow and stern were decorated with bright enamel paint and real gold leaf. Thirty-two shields, painted yellow and black, just like the ones on the *Gokstad*, decorated her sides.

As the day wore on the sightseers dropped away, and finally the last of the guests moved to the *Leif Erikson* to return to port. *Viking's* crew decided to pull the small boats, which they had been towing, aboard. Dinner was made in a pot hanging from the mast, and everyone looked hopefully forward to an exciting journey.

As nightfall drew near, the tent, which would be their only protection from the weather, was set up in the middle of the boat. There were no beds of bunks. Each man had a reindeer skin for a mattress, placed directly onto the deck boards. On top of that, two blankets sewn together into a sort of basic sleeping bag. The men used their boots for pillows, or commandeered one of the reindeer-hair bags. In spite of the primitive conditions, they slept well.

On May, the passed Fair Isle, between the Orkneys and Scotland, where the Spanish Armada had run aground in 1588. Rasmussen noted the lighthouse there, atop a large stony hill, and behind that, beautiful green fields. The crew released two carrier pigeons to transmit news of their journey so far, but the birds disappeared and did not make it home.

ON THE ATLANTIC

The difference in the sea was noticeable when *Viking* reached the Atlantic. Larger waves moved against the ship, and soon a gale was blowing. The men ran the mechanical pump steadily since the choppy water came up over the rear of the ship.

Then the mechanical pump broke. The crew took it apart and repaired it, but it broke again. Water was coming in steadily. Finally, the men discarded their modern pump, took up some of the deck boards, and simply bailed with buckets.

In this storm *Viking* proved herself a gallant ship. She was undaunted by the tall waves, facing each one from the best possible angle. Water came in, but not nearly as much as the crew had expected in such an open boat. The man at the helm reported that her unorthodox steering was the best he had ever used.

All through the night the ship and her crew battled the storm, and when it was over, the sailors declared their complete faith in *Viking*. "A better ship is not afloat in salt water!" declared one.

By dawn, the ship had been bailed dry, the storm was nearly over, and they were making 7 or 8 miles an hour under full sail.

Rasmussen tells us "She had kissed the seas as only a Viking ship can."

The sailors were actually having an easier time than they had anticipated. In fact, the only person suffering was Frantzen, the steward/cook. Since the open boat had no galley, pantry, shelves or tables, all cooking had to be done standing over an open, smoky fire. It was impossible to keep plates or utensils clean and dry. One of the steward's jobs was to sleep next to the stove to keep the cranky thing going. Preparing food seemed like the hardest job on the ship.

For this reason, Rasmussen was ordered to take the cook's place for several days. He didn't like the job, but tried to do it with a good will. After all, orders were orders, and his crewmates had to eat. "Appetites like Vikings!" he complained in his memoir.

Early the next evening another gale started up. This time the waves were even higher. As the wind rose, they spotted a schooner bearing down on them. The captain ordered a change in sails to let the other ship go by, then called when it was close enough, "Can you take mail?" This was a standard courtesy at sea. With no radio to offer a progress report to those back home, ships heading into port often carried mail for outward-bound ship.

In this case, the answer was "No!" The schooner was running too fast to stop, but offered to report that the *Viking* was still doing well, and what her position was.

And then they were in the storm. Every hour the wind rose. All hands were on deck. The Viking made a terrible noise, groaning in every seam as the pressure on her mast and sides caused every joint to flex and move.

The waves grew as tall as mountains. *Viking* rushed toward each one at top speed, but was unable to come over the crests. She was too short.

The crew tried to adjust her approach to the waves by using the sea anchor. They launched it with great difficulty, fighting the wind and water. But it did not work. The crew hauled it back in. Then they tried launching a buoy. This did no good either.

This was what *Viking* had been built for, though her builders had not realized at the time. She could not defeat the waves, but she faced each one, at exactly the right angle, with no help at all from the man at the helm. The crew were amazed. They literally did not understand how a boat so small and so strangely built could survive a storm of this magnitude.

With a lesser ship, the crew's loved ones might never have known their fate, just a sighting from a schooner who reporting *Viking*'s last position before the storm hit.

This was the storm that changed the feelings of her crew from respect to love. They loved this ship. She brought them through in perfect safety. Though wet and cold, they were men of the sea, and they could ask no more.

A CELEBRATION

For several days the *Viking* crew enjoyed smooth sailing. Rasmussen went back to his job as bosun and helmsman, and the cook was cooking once again.

On the Seventeenth of May, the crew was ready for a celebration. It was Constitution Day, the anniversary of the signing of Norway's proclamation of herself an independent nation. The weather was beautiful, and all the crew had to do was adjust the sails as finely as possible to increase speed. Under the tent, which was still in place in the middle of the ship, the crew sat, talking about their homeland, their friends, and their gallant *Viking*.

In the evening, Captain Andersen invited everyone into the rear of the ship, usually considered "officers only" territory. He had brought rum and cigars. The cook mixed everyone a hot toddy, and they smoked and drank while the captain made a speech praising each man's hard work and bravery.

Then he suggested that each of the crew make a speech. Public speeches were a popular form of entertainment, but this was very much "performance on command." Some were eager to speak, but for the ones who were too shy, leading a song was an acceptable substitute. Some men spoke of the exotic places they had been, such as New Guinea and California. Others told funny stories about their early training as sailors. One fellow made an impassioned political speech and pounded on the chest they were using for a table until his hand bled.

But much of the talk was about *Viking* herself, her building, her seaworthiness, and what a good representative she was of their mother country. Every man knew that the eyes of the world would be upon them. The talk and song went on until 10:00 at night, and after a hard day at work, a little sleep in the tent was very welcome.

During the night they had enjoyed a fresh breeze that kept the ship moving at a brisk pace, but then they fell into the bane of sailing ships – a calm. For days they waited for some sort of breeze.

On May 19th, a wind came, accompanied by mist and wet. The breeze slowly rose to another gale, and everyone was cold and uncomfortable. But *Viking* remained as reliable as ever, offering safety from the sea and making the men feel blessed.

At noon the next day the lookout sighted a large steamship heading right toward them. They did not want to miss this opportunity, as they had the last one, and immediately raised a signal asking the steamer to stop for letters.

When the reply signal was, "Yes" the Viking crew lowered one of the small boats, and Simonsen and Rasmussen rowed first Mate Gundersen over to the other ship, the *Amarynthia*.

The steamship's passengers were excited to see the strange-looking *Viking,* and wondered aloud what kind of ship she was and where she came from. Even the Norwegian flag, flying from *Viking*'s stern post was not much help. Many people guessed that she was a German ship.

The Norwegians dropped off their letters, and took *Amarynthia's* letters in turn. Rasmussen somehow got a look at one of the letters, and recorded a snippet of it in his book:

> Captain of *Amarynthia:* On May 20, about 12:15 p.m., I observed something that looked like a ship's boat, but I later thought it to a raft. As we came nearer, I found it to be the most remarkable example of a ship I had ever seen in the Atlantic. The *Viking* signaled that it wanted to send a boat over to us, so I stopped. The mate came aboard with letters and a request to send a telegram to the committee as soon as we arrived at our destination., which was done. The mate also informed me that the *Viking* had managed very well though two storms and all on board were well.

Once the small boat was settled back in Viking's stern, they went off, sailing into the wind.

On the 22nd, crewmember Løkke became ill with flu-like symptoms, headaches, body aches, and a high fever. It must have been hard for him. *Viking* was strong and safe, but she had no comfortable or dry place to sleep, and most of the modern remedies had not yet been invented. Løkke made the best of it.

While trying to fit him out with a slightly more comfortable bed, the crew realized that the reindeer-hair pillows, which they had been using as fenders – padding to soften impact between two ships, were dragging behind *Viking* on a rope, some of them ripped open. The important thing became taking care of the equipment.

The fog was so dense that it was hard to see from one end of *Viking* to the other. So, in addition to his other problems, Løkke had to listen to the continual blowing of his ship's foghorn. In the low visibility, this was the only way for *Viking* to announcer her presence, and avoid possibly being run down by a larger ship.

The next day they did, in fact, almost run into another steam ship, this one from the same shipping company as the *Amarynthia*.

But unlike her sister ship, this vessel did not have time to visit or take letters. They only promised to report Viking's position, and then went on in a terrible hurry.

Viking's crew kept trying to arrange for more comfortable sleeping arrangements, now using spare deck boards and supply chests to build primitive bunks under the tent. But sea-spray and mist still came in, leaving everything wet.

They were very far north, with no source of heat except the smoky cook-fire, keeping warm with wool clothing, wool blankets and reindeer hides. Everyone had ear-aches from the cold. Ordinary tasks sometimes made the men's hands crack and bleed.

Yet what they remember was a sense of wonder and beauty. The sunset on May 25th was gorgeous enough to be remarked upon years later. Curious whales surrounded *Viking*. Icebergs began to loom over them, some as large as Norway's mountains. The cold coming off these mountains of ice was intense, and the sailors were keenly aware that much more ice lurked beneath the surface, enough to wreck any ship. Nineteen years later, one of these icebergs would sink the unsinkable *Titanic*.

The prime activity for the crew was scraping debris off the ship. I once asked a Navy friend "Why do sailors always swab the deck? There can't be any dirt out there."

His reply is that a person might wish for common dirt, because what gets on a ship is fish poo, bird droppings, and rotting fish bits that some other fish let float to the surface while eating. *Viking's* crew wanted her to present a neat appearance to those who would be seeing her, so they spent hours every day leaning over the sides, scraping debris off as far down as they could reach. In the worst weather, they cleaned the parts of the ship under the tent.

On Friday the 26th, they sighted a lighthouse in the distance. Also, four icebergs.

On the 27th, they came close to Baccalieu Island, Cape Spear, and St. Johns, some of the easternmost parts of North America, in Newfoundland, Canada. They had made it.

The wind died here, and *Viking* drifted, frustrating the crew, who very much wanted to get off the boat for a while, buy supplies, and telegram their families back home.

That afternoon, a tugboat, the *D. P. Ingerham,* came out to ask questions and offer assistance. While the Vikings had been looking at the land, the landsmen had been looking back. *Viking*'s red and white striped sail and short mast had confused them. They wondered if *Viking* was a wreck with a broken mast, coming in on a sail made from rags.

Captain Andersen invited the tugboat's crew to come over, and the *Ingerham*'s captain and machinist were very excited to do so. The machinist especially so. He had worked on the sea for forty years, and had never yet set foot on a true sailing ship.

As he looked over this very unusual vessel, he explained to the Norwegians how he had been born on the north coast of England, where he had grown up hearing tales of the Vikings, their ships, and the terrible raids that had sowed fear in the whole region. As child he had not believed the stories, thinking they were more like fairy tales. Now he was standing on a real Viking ship with a real Viking crew. His entire world-view had been changed.

The tugboat left with letters, telegrams, and reports of a most unusual ship with all well on board.

Viking continued her struggle with the weather and the wind. The crew was still chilled by nightly mists. The wind refused to blow. A cold rain started.

But the crew was adept at remaining cheerful. They met fellow Norwegians of the *Martha,* out of Kristiania, under Captain Nelson. When wind allowed the two ships had a short sailing race, and then shared a meal, with *Viking* providing pancakes, meat patties and Viking beer, which was remarked upon as being excellent. On the relatively calm sea, Viking was even able to produce an excellent cup of coffee. Then the Martha headed back to Norway, leaving *Viking* with no favorable wind, and a trip before her

They observed the many boats fishing in the area and threw out a few lines of their own. In no time, they had dozens of fish. The crew cleaned fish until midnight, and the steward, Frantzen, cooked fried fish, smoked fish, boiled fish and fish stew until the crew claimed that they were turning into halibut.

May 31 began another period of dead calm, and the hard work of cleaning went on. During this time Rasmussen decided to replace the white jib sail that he had rigged at the beginning of the journey with a red-and-white-striped one that would match the mainsail. The decision may have been inspired by the earlier confusion about *Viking* being a wreck with a rag sail. It may also have been inspired by the fact that they had the fabric available. *Viking* had left Norway with a spare red and white mainsail, and there had been absolutely no use for it on the voyage. Rasmussen set up in the rear of the ship, outside the tent, where the light was best, and began to cut and sew.

His job was made more complicated by the fact that the fabric had been donated, and the manufacturer had decided to add a little publicity by stamping his company name all over the fabric. This simply would not do. Viking was a historical expedition, not an advertising display. Rasmussen carefully cut out all the stamps, and began to carefully, neatly sew the remaining fabric into a sail that was both functional and beautiful.

All the men were still suffering from the cold and damp. Rasmussen's hands bled, but he felt he was working on a matter of national pride for his homeland, as well as a project that would be judged by other sailors. Water dripping off his face, he doggedly remained in the mist and rain, sewing.

They continued to wait for a favorable wind, riding with the current to make any tiny amount of progress and making the most of any breeze. On June 7th, an American schooner swooped down on them, and Captain Andersen hailed them. The schooner was a fishing vessel out of Gloucester, manned primarily by Scandinavians, most of them Norwegian. Fourteen men came aboard *Viking*, talked about the local fishing, and shared *Viking*'s beer.

The lack of wind continued, as did the cleaning. Without wind, a trip that could have been completed in two days would take weeks. The only consolation was that Viking was finally clean enough to win her crew's approval. Even the mast and the oars were shining! The crew, however, had not bathed or changed their clothes since Norway.

The dragon head and tail had been taken down once they were out at sea. This was a common practice for ships with intricately carved figureheads. Now was the time to set them back up. Small boats were all around, it was time for the newly-cleaned *Viking* to show off all her beauty.

1925 postage stamp featuring *Viking. Notice the striped foresail*

The dragon had been stored carefully, wrapped in wool to pad it and then sewen into an oiled canvas cover, which was then painted to make it even more waterproof. Still, the crew was nervous. Everything in the boat had been banged around in the storms, soaked with salt water and nearly frozen. Would the decorations still be presentable? But the care given by her loving crew had stood *Viking*'s ornaments in good stead. Both head and tail were almost as lovely as when they had been brought aboard. A few nicks were only to be expected.

Now was the time to lighten *Viking*'s load as well. Many of the zinc boxes which had held provisions were damaged beyond repair – smashed, full of holes, literally torn apart by the elements. Over the side they went. Along with them went the temperamental mechanical pump. Shelters that had been built in the bow and stern were also ripped up and tossed overboard. What had seemed like a good idea in the shipyard had not worked at all at sea. The structures had only collected seawater, to such an extent that the tent had provided better shelter.

With warmer, dryer weather, the tent was also taken down and stowed. Now *Viking* was looking her best.

On June 14th a passing schooner let them know they were expected in Newport, Rhode Island. They had been sighted, and a party was being prepared.

Now that they finally had some wind, Captain Andersen had hoped to go a farther fifty miles down the coast to New London, in Connecticut. This had been their destination two weeks ago, before the wind had given out. Though it took until 4:00 pm the next day, they pressed on until they arrived at their destination.

As soon as *Viking*'s anchor dropped, a swarm of boats surrounded her, full of people who wanted to see *Viking*, and possibly come aboard. Captain Andersen allowed a few, including reporters from New York and Boston.

The visitors brought correspondence, including an invitation from the recently-bypassed Newport. Captain Andersen remembered that this was a good-will mission, relented and replied that they would come back.

While Andersen was sending his reply, *Viking*'s crew was dealing with the fans and reporters. They discovered that these Americans were fascinated by the Norwegian coins in their pockets. If only they had known, they might have brought more and made quite a profit. Already the crowd was saying that if these men and this boat could cross the Atlantic, then it was completely possible that Leif Eriksen had done so.

FIRST RECEPTION

On July 14th, *Viking* was on her way to Rhode Island, pulled by a tugboat so she would not need to battle a contrary current. It took only a few hours to reach the harbor, where they were immediately surrounded by a small fleet of sightseeing boats. Newport's Fort Adams let loose a thunderous salutation of cannons, and it seemed that every gun in the city was fired.

As soon as *Viking* dropped anchor, hundreds of boats and people crowded close wanting to see her. The crew was invited to a dinner hosted by the local Norwegian Committee. It would be their first meal in America – a hasty one, since they had to rush back and guard the ship.

The next order of business was baths for the men. They had not washed since Norway. After bathing, shampoos and beard trims, they could hardly recognize each other. They slept that night on *Viking*.

The next day, the 15th, *Viking* was towed to the naval yard to have her bottom cleaned in one of the slips. However, *Viking* was so much wider than other ships her size that it wasn't possible. The crew had to do it the old-fashioned way, by dragging her up onto the beach. The navy men did help – more scraping.

At 1:00 pm the church bells began to ring, signifying the beginning of the town's festivities. Though it was a Thursday, the town had come to a standstill to see *Viking* and her Viking crew.

And they were Vikings. In the nomenclature of ships, the crew goes by the name of the ship. So, if the crew of the *Titanic* had ever made it to shore, they would be referred to as Titanics. The crew of the *John L. Sullivan* would be "Sullivans," or singularly a "Sullivan." The men who had crossed the sea in *Viking* really were Vikings.

A steamboat full of passengers had come all the way from Boston. The Vikings were already dirty again from their work, but went aboard anyway, leaving only one man – and the navy – to guard their ship.

The local Norwegian-Americans offered a speech praising the accomplishments of the visitors and Mother Norway. First Mate Gundersen expressed thanks and praised *Viking*, saying the old-time Norwegians knew how to build ships. He also offered a toast to the Norwegian-Americans.

Later they left to a local rowing club, where they finally had a chance to wash again. The 1890s was not a spic-and-span era, the Vikings were still wearing the clothes they had crossed the Atlantic in.

The next stop was in Touro Park, to a round tower called at the time "the Old Norwegian Mill." The structure, a not-quite-round stone tower which was centuries old and was rumored to have been a fortress built by Viking explorers to defend themselves from Native Americans.

The Vikings were deeply moved by what they believed may have been evidence of the struggles of their ancestors. Captain

Andersen went so far as to climb a tree to get a good photograph.

Old Newport Tower circa 1894, photo courtesy of Wikimedia Commons

In the style of the day, each of the Vikings was presented with one of the tower's rocks as a memento, as well as a model of the structure.

The history of the structure was never certain. Modern carbon dating indicates the tower was built no earlier than the 1600s, though local legend persists in calling it a Viking structure.

That night there was a dinner in the Mason's Lodge, with many speeches. To modern folks, hours of after-dinner speeches sounds torturous, but this was an age when people were willing to travel for miles and pay money to hear a good speaker.

Rooms had been reserved for them at a local hotel. This would be their first night away from *Viking*. But the next morning they were back at the navy base scraping the dirt from their beloved ship once again.

BROOKLYN

They were scheduled to arrive in New York on the 17th. Captain Andersen went on ahead by train, and the crew put *Viking* back in the water and sailed. At last the wind was strong and favorable, and if the waves were a little rough, it was nothing to what they had already endured. They sailed through Long Island Sound amid hundreds of pleasure craft, to the din of bells, horns and gunshots.

Viking was looking her best. The Norwegian flag flew from a flagpole in the rear, the American flag from one near the bow. A Viking banner featuring a raven topped the mast. Silk banners filled in between. The golden dragon head and tail gleamed in the sun, and all 32 yellow and black Viking shields decorated her sides.

Large yachts surrounded Cony Island, looking like floating palaces. One of the largest held the reception committee, including many of the most important Norwegians in New York, New York's mayor, Thomas Gilroy, Norway's Commissioner of the Chicago World's Fair, presidents of local rowing and yacht clubs, and *Viking's* Captain Andersen.

The warship *Minatomah* arrived to escort them through the crowd of boats. Music followed them, a significant detail in a time when music was always "live" and required a band. A new, larger tugboat came up to speed *Viking* along. In the crush to get near *Viking*, several pleasure boats tipped over, but since no-one drowned, it did not seem like a major issue.

New York gave a thunderous twenty-one cannon salute as *Viking* passed the Statue of Liberty. Then *Viking*'s crew lowered her sail and began to row. They were still in their wool clothing, in a much warmer climate, and using oars which had been designed 1000 years ago – they missed the modern improvements., and were soon sweating and exhausted. Finally, they were simply towed into harbor.

In New York, they planned to stay on land for a few days. The Vikings chose a hotel, then marched to Prospect Hall for the next event honoring them, the Raven banner carried in front

This was a four-hour dinner, excellent food, hostesses in Norwegian national costume, and more speeches. After that, music and dancing until 3:30 am. When some of the men tried to beg off, pleading inexperience at dancing or just plain exhaustion, Captain Andersen insisted that they all stay together in a group. This was to prove a very wise decision.

When the party was finally over, the Vikings did all leave together, along with many of the party's guests who happened to be going the same direction.

Rasmussen describes what happened next. One of the Vikings, 39-year-old Nygaard, was set upon by a strange man who appeared to be drunk. After landing a punch or two and pushing Nygaard down, the drunk man ran off. Nygaard wanted to chase him, but was stopped by Rasmussen and the others, who insisted that they were "peaceful Vikings" and it would not be dignified to carry on fighting.

They crossed into Brooklyn, the location of their hotel, and were walking quietly along when the drunken man came back and started ranting and shouting at them. Once again, the Vikings made no reply, other than to tell him to go home. Then the police descended.

A policeman attacked Rasmussen, hitting him with a nightstick, then kicking him so that he fell down. When Rasmussen asked what he was doing, the policeman hit him in the head so hard he was knocked out.

Captain Andersen came back from the front of the straggling line and attempted to stop the assault, only to be repeatedly struck by another policeman. Every time he attempted to find out what was going on, he was struck again. When Rasmussen woke up and tried to get to his feet, he was also struck repeatedly.

The guests, Vikings, and other people gathered around shouting at the police to stop, but it only caused the officers to strike into the crowd. Rasmussen finally got hold of the nightstick, which caused the policeman to punch him twice in the face. Finally, fearing for his life, Rasmussen told the policeman, "If you don't stop hitting me, I'll see to it you are never able to use that stick again." This finally stopped the assault.

Captain Andersen spotted the original troublemaker standing nearby, and told the police to arrest him. The response was, "We'll arrest whomever we choose!"

Apparently, this did not include the troublemaker. Five of the Vikings were shoved into a police wagon, but when the guests tried to join them, they were pushed away.

Rasmussen was suffering from a concussion. He remembers being taken to the Hamilton Avenue Police station, where their personal possessions, including their watches, were taken from them, and then pushed into a cell. Rasmussen lay down on the floor.

The other Vikings arrived and managed to get in to talk to their captain. Andersen was protesting their treatment, telling the desk Sargent that the Vikings had done nothing wrong, but was met with smug approval of the policemen's actions, along with the question "Do you think you can do as you please in this country?"

When Gundersen reached his captain for instructions, Andersen told him, "Go to the Mayor of New York, thank him for his invitation to meet with him at 11:00 today, and tell him what has happened, and ask him to excuse us if we cannot make the appointment. Then go back to *Viking* and sail her back to Norway."

This is a quote from Rasmussen's account, and it seems a very strange set of instructions. Did the concussed Rasmussen mis-remember? Or was Captain Andersen perhaps suffering from a blow to the head as well?

Or perhaps it was intended as a veiled threat? If the first trip was to New York's Mayor, the curt message would have caused questions, and if the answer to those questions was "I've been instructed to take *Viking* back to Norway," it signaled a public-relations disaster. Thousands upon thousands of very important people were waiting for *Viking* and her crew, and if the good-will mission was called off while the boat and crew were under the protection of New York's mayor, the mayor would be to blame. Viewed this way, Captain Andersen's instructions may have been genius, words that would not have alerted any guards to what he was hinting at, while setting into motion an official rescue mission. The Viking crew were shoved into tiny holding cells, without so much as a drop of water. The Norwegian-American businessman Helmen Johnson was at the desk, trying to get Captain Andersen released on bond, but the Captain refused to be parted from his men.

Finally, at 7:00 am, the doors were opened, and the Vikings were formally charged with drunken and disorderly conduct. Captain Andresen refused to sign the charges, fearing to incriminate himself. One by one the Vikings described themselves as being perfectly sober, walking quietly to their hotel. Rasmussen, still with a ringing headache, was accused as the others were, with the added charge of having torn the coat of the policeman who had beaten him.

Then the Vikings were forced out of the building, into a waiting police van. They were then taken from the holding cells to the courthouse, and shoved into a long, narrow cell with no window, only a small hatch in the ceiling. A dozen or so prisoners were already in the cell, and as they waited, more and more men were crammed in, until the room could literally hold no more. When day began to heat up, men began to faint, thought the press was so close that they had to remain on their feet. The unconscious men were removed.

Eventually court started, and conscious men were led into court one by one. Some were released with a fine, but those who did not have the money, or who had a harsher sentence, were brought back to the cell.

Captain Andersen had asked for a quick hearing, citing his appointment with the mayor, but he was given no consideration. Finally, the Captain was called. He was out a short time, then was returned and Rasmussen was called.

Rasmussen was fighting unconsciousness, due both to his head wound and to the foul conditions in the cell. In the courtroom Judge Tighe asked if he was ready to plead guilty.

"What are the charges?"

Now, in addition to being drunk and disorderly, and tearing the policeman's coat, Rasmussen was charged with having stolen one of the watches that had been taken from the Vikings. When he produced his own watch, which had been missed in the muddle, it only caused more confusion. Rasmussen asserted his innocence and was sent back to the cell.

One by one, the Vikings were promised their freedom in return for a confession, and one by one they asserted their innocence and were sent back.

Meanwhile, Captain Andersen was trying to find out if they could be released on bail. A sum of $200 was set – each. This sum represented about 4 months' salary for a skilled sailor, and seemed impossible. But The bail bondsman was still there, ready to arrange bail for everyone, if the Captain would not accept it for himself alone. After carefully making sure that they were not admitting to guilt, they each signed and, were finally allowed to leave. The full bond would be required if they failed to appear.

Upon the request that trial be soon, to accommodate the Vikings' schedule, Judge Tighe said that it was none of his business, that they were guilty, and would have to deal with the consequences. As the Viking were leaving the building, he was also heard to remark to a subordinate, "These people own New York, and now they think they can take a slice of Brooklyn too."

As the Vikings exited the building, they were met with applause and cheers. A crowd had gathered in support of the crew, and they followed as the men marched to New York's City Hall, where they were greeted by the secretary of the Reception Committee, a Mr. Randall. The Mayor arrived, gave a welcoming speech, and shook the hands of each of the Vikings. "I'm deeply sorry about the treatment you have been given, and I am sure you are completely innocent. In order for you to see that New York is one city and Brooklyn is another, (Brooklyn would not become a borough of New York until 1898.) and that we sincerely wish you welcome, I invite you to be the guests of New York while you are here. You may stay in any hotel and travel wherever you want. New York will pay all expenses. We do this to show that we believe you have been treated unjustly."

He shook hands all around again, and then ushered in the press.

The rest of the day was spent sightseeing and meeting prominent New Yorkers. The Stock Exchange stopped trading while the Vikings visited.

What the crewmen really enjoyed, however, was a trip to a Turkish bath. This was a public bathing facility with soaking pools at various temperatures, facilities for swimming, and steam rooms. After all the days and weeks of hard work and sweat, it must have been heaven.

While all of this had been taking place one man after another had always been standing guard on *Viking*. When the trial came due, Rasmussen was on guard duty, so we have a summary from his point of view, and reports from the *New York Times*.

On Tuesday, Captain Andersen, with his lawyer Mr. Raymert, along with first mate Gundersen, took the Vikings' complaint to Mayor Boody of Brooklyn. They received a very dignified apology from the mayor. (According to the Brooklyn

Daily Eagle Almanac, New York's mayor had spoken to him the day before.) When Mr. Gundersen asked if the policemen would be punished, he was told that while the mayor did not have authority to interfere directly with the police, he would see to it that the police commissioner looked into it. Captain Andersen also made a formal complaint about their trial being put off until Monday. All in all, he and his men had not only been hurt, they had been insulted.

At about this time, Judge Tighe and the Chief of Police arrived. The judge had lost his contemptuous tone. "I have gotten the worst of this affair," he complained. "The newspapers have made life difficult for me. I hardly know what to do. What do you want?"

Captain Andersen reiterated his request for an immediate trial.

"Very well," the judge replied. "But Captain Andersen and his men will have to appear."

"Not only they, but two hundred and fifty friends who are willing to testify that the Captain Andersen and his men are blameless," was the retort of the lawyer.

The New York Times reported the events with a strong bias toward Captain Andersen and his crew. They were "sturdy Vikings", while Judge Tighe's shady financial entanglements with taverns and prizefighting was highlighted, as well as his small physical size and lack of athletic achievements. The paper also gave plenty of space to the judge's assentation that sailing *Viking* across the ocean was no great achievement, "Put a boat like that in the water and it will float like a chip (of wood)" Judge Tighe was quoted as saying.

The trial was moved up to 8:00 am on Wednesday, and all the crew except those on guard duty were at the courthouse, supported by cheering crowds.

The drunken fellow who had started it all was not present. The policemen were not present (on vacation was the handy excuse.) Without them, the Vikings were immediately acquitted. Captain Andersen made a short speech stating that he and his men had not received restitution, only the barest justice which they deserved. Tighe had been humiliated. He slunk off without a word. Days later, he was still receiving letters of condemnation. The Norwegian community, instrumental in getting him elected to his position, was indignant and wrathful.

The mayor and other city officials wanted to see *Viking*, and they were soon on board, having their pictures taken and being toasted with Norwegian wine.

Shortly afterward, Captain Andersen left for Washington D.C., where he met with President Grover Cleveland.

One wonders why Tighe and the police were willing to take on the enormously popular Norwegians. From meetings with mayors, to the shouting crowds in the streets, it must have been obvious that *Viking* and her crew were immensely popular. Perhaps the judge was jealous? His comments to the press that he did not hold the achievements of the crew in high regard may hint at jealousy, especially since the papers note that he himself had been a common sailor early in life, and was now a member of a local yacht club. Whatever the reason, with his voting base enraged, Tighe probably paid the full price for his foolishness.

ON TO THE ERIE

Before they set sail up the Hudson River, the Vikings finally had a chance to go shopping. Each man was given $12, and the whole crew went out to buy new uniforms. They selected blue pants and jackets, grey shirts, and fashionable straw hats.

Monday, June 26th, was the date set for their departure. Some American students, some of them from local rowing clubs, volunteered to come along and help with the oars, and two professional seamen also joined, to help the beleaguered steward.

Unfortunately, the tugboat which had been promised by the Navy while Captain Andersen was in Washington failed to appear. Communications with the Brooklyn navy Yard confirmed that the boat would not be available until the following day. The weather was unpleasant: the wind blowing a gale, black clouds and rain. Captain Andersen decided to head up the Hudson on their own, and spend the night in Yonkers. It would not speed their journey, but would allow *Viking* to show her capabilities to the crowds of sightseers who had come out to cheer her, in spite of the weather.

Viking raised her mainsail and impressed everyone with her speed.

Yonkers offered loud hurrahs and salutes as well. The newly installed assistant Vikings may have been a little uncomfortable with their new accommodations, which were still hardly luxurious, but the old hands reveled in the steward's latest gadget – a kerosene stove that did not smoke.

The tugboat found them early the next morning – early enough that the American students thought they should still be asleep. But the day was already beginning to look beautiful, with fresh breezes that chased away the clouds. The tugboat offered a tow line, and soon the ship was off, being towed at the impressive speed of eleven miles an hour.

All along the river, homes and boats displayed the American flag, and sometimes the Norwegian flag as well. The Vikings enjoyed views of the lovely country along the river, and land which at this time was filled with small, prosperous farms.

As they passed West Point military academy, the recruits came out to offer hearty cheers, answered by the American students, who took up the task of replying to the hurrahs as if it was their duty.

A two-hour stop at the town of Newburgh left just enough time for loading provisions, touring George Washington's former headquarters, and breakfast.

Next stop was Albany. Though the crew never set foot off the ship, they were treated to a fireworks display. The government tugboat needed to return home, but a steamship named *Priam* offered to take them as far as Troy, where the Erie Canal begins.

Rasmussen was enjoying it all – the hearty greetings, the New York scenery, the food, the speeches, the fireworks. But he recounts in his journal that the thing which stirred his heart the most was a choir of children on one of the boats, wearing Norwegian national costumes, and singing. It reminded him so sharply of the sound of his own four children saying "Goodbye Papa" that he was moved to tears.

The Erie Canal had been built in the early part of the century, and completed in 1825. Despite its importance in opening up the West, and its place in song and folklore, the entire length of the canal is in the state of New York. It runs 363 miles from the Hudson River in Albany to Lake Erie in Buffalo. The canal created a water route from New York City and the Atlantic Ocean to the Great Lakes. When completed, it was the second longest canal in the world (after the Grand Canal in China). Boats and barges took the canal west, and once in Lake Erie, they could use natural features of rivers and lakes to reach any of the Great Lakes. *Viking*'s final destination, the Chicago Exposition, was right on the shore of Lake Michigan.

The problem was that the land rises about 600 feet from the Hudson River to Lake Erie. If the builders had simply dug an open canal, water from the lake would have flowed toward the Hudson River until the Great Lakes were at the same level as the Atlantic Ocean – in other words, forever. This was solved by installing locks along the route.

A lock is a fixed chamber along the waterway, used for raising and lowering watercraft between stretches of water of different levels. A boat or barge enters the lock, the lock is sealed, and then pumps raise or lower the water inside the lock to raise or lower the boat. Locks in 1893 could handle up to 12 feet of lift, so seventy-three locks were required along the canal.

On the sea, *Viking* was relatively small. In the canal system, she was huge. At 73 feet long and 17 feet wide, she barely fit into the eighty-one-foot locks, and even the turns of the waterway were difficult for her to handle.

A tugboat, the *Netty,* had been assigned to tow her, but since it had not arrived, a team of horses was hitched up instead. The animals were used to moving heavier freight, and they started at a brisk pace. This had *Viking* moving too fast for her own good. As the canal made a sharp bend, the ship risked a collision with the embankment. The crew leaped into the canal and onto the bank and pushed with all their might. Their quick actions lessened the blow. The embankment took a chip of wood off *Viking*'s bow, but the damage was only cosmetic.

Due to the low bridges ahead, the crew had already taken down the beautiful dragonhead and tail, and used the hinge at the base of the mast to lower it. Still people came out to see her. A crowd formed at the first lock, pointing and shouting that she must be a Spanish ship – no, Norwegian. The flags were similar. News of *Viking*'s journey had gone on before her, and people who had read about her story teased those who didn't already know.

By noon, they were at the fifteenth lock. Here they waited for the *Netty* to reach them, and made use of the new kerosene stove to cook lunch. The new hands wanted to take the helm, but she needed an experienced hand to get her through the wide S-turns.

The tugboat arrived, and with it pulling, speed increased to about six miles an hour, which felt dangerous. Now the canal was full of traffic. The tugboat overtook slower moving barges, and strings of barges were also going the opposite direction.

Viking's helmsman stood on a makeshift scaffold for a better view of the canal.

At midnight, when the watch changed, the crew commented among themselves about the speed, and how the tugboat kept hauling along on its merry way, in spite of the increased traffic.

At 1:00 am, it happened. On another wide bend, the tugboat drifted out into the center of the canal, just as a string of barges came up from the opposite direction. The last barge in the string also swung wide, and with a crash, tugboat and barge collided at full speed.

Shouts and confusion. The tugboat struck the barge so hard she rebounded right into *Viking*'s side. The crew thought their beloved ship would be crushed.

Fortunately, the blow hit next to the steering oar, right on the extra-strong rib which supported the steering mechanism. The two-and-a-half-inch thick oaken plank split and was driven inward a full two inches, but it held.

The tugboat was in worse shape, with a gaping hole in her bow, driven all the way up onto the bank.

Captain Andersen awoke and rushed forward to see what he could do. *Viking* was lying crosswise in the channel, with her stern driven onto the bank. The next passing boat would surely strike her again.

Rasmussen and two of the new men leaped off and began pushing, trying to get *Viking* back into the water. At first it was no use. They strained and grunted to no effect. Then, movement! With redoubled strength, the men pushed, and *Viking* was free!

The tugboat had a three-foot hole in her bow, water gushing into her. If not for her position on the bank, she would have sunk. After their own craft was safe, the Vikings went over to see if they could help. They found a ship that could no longer move, and a very contrite crew. The American students began shouting, blaming the tugboat crew for the accident.

The towline was tangled in the tugboat's propeller, and had to be cut. The Vikings asked for a knife to cut the rope, but the tugboat's crew was afraid of the students to give them one. The Norwegians produced their own knife and cut themselves free.

With no other means of mobility, members of the crew took hold of the towline and began to walk down the path usually used by horses, hauling *Viking* along by pure manpower. It was exhausting work, but they were determined to keep moving.

The men pulled all night. A team of horses was finally brought up at about dawn, and the tired men could rest. The day was lovely, the countryside beautiful, but no one seemed to notice *Viking*, and the crew, already used to adulation everywhere they went, felt the loss.

At the town of Canajoharie, near the thirty-first lock, *Viking*'s notoriety finally caught up with her again. Thousands come to see the ship. This was the new normal in the lives of the crew, and they were happy. Captain Andersen went ahead to find another tugboat.

Why was *Viking* so popular? Part of the reason may have been the high number of Norwegian-Americans in the area. Some of it was undoubtedly the novelty of something new, in a time when small-town life was beginning to seem dull. More may have been that the original concept was right; Americans are impressed by bravery.

But even more was probably *Viking*'s association with the Columbian Exposition. This was America's first such event. News of it was in every newspaper, on every tongue. And though millions of people would eventually see the great event, millions more would not, held back by family or business obligations, or simple lack of money. *Viking* was a bit of the Exhibition come to them, and for this reason she was thrilling.

The horses dragged *Viking* slowly along. At the town of Little Falls, more thousands covered each side of the canal, calling "Welcome Vikings!" The crew noticed that even this small town had electric lights, still a bit of a novelty.

The weather continued to be lovely. A tugboat, arranged by Captain Andersen, came to speed them on their way. It was owned by a local merchant and steered by his daughter. This young woman was skilled, careful, and tenacious. She took due care, both of her father's boat and of *Viking*. The crew praised her highly, and wished aloud that she had been the one guiding the tugboat they had started out with.

Viking reached the forty-sixth lock and the town of Syracuse at 6:00 pm on June 30th, and stopped for a dinner held in their honor at a large hotel. Afterward there were more speeches, and one of the local ladies sang in Norwegian for the group. The crew were back in their ship by midnight, however, and continued on.

Who should they meet in Rochester, but the *Nina*, the *Pinta* and the *Santa Maria*? These replicas had been built in Spain for the Exposition, but the Spanish had not dared to sail the primitive boats across the Atlantic. These vessels had been towed by a warship, and the Norwegians got in some barbed comments about how much better the tenth century Vikings were as boat builders, compared to the fifteenth century Spanish.

Enormous masses met them in Rochester, crowding the bridges and pelting them with flowers, until *Viking* smelled like a garden, instead of a boat full of sweaty men. One persistent admirer ran ahead from bridge to bridge, waving a large Norwegian flag and shouting, "Welcome countrymen!"

Nina, Pinta and *Santa Maria* at the Columbian Exposition, 1893

They passed the last of the locks and arrived at Buffalo on July 3rd.

A day of festivities had been planned, but they were still trying to make up time for the delay in Brooklyn. The governor of New York State greeted them, and the mayor of Philadelphia. The Vikings met with the welcoming committee, toured city hall, and listened to speeches, this time including jokes about how they had almost been wrecked on the canal.

Originally, a side-trip for the crew had been planned, so they could see Niagara Falls, only 17 miles away. But there was no time. Even if the rest of the crew had gone, Rasmussen would have needed to stay behind. He needed to ready *Viking* to sail again, this time across the Great Lakes.

SAILING THE LAKES

Now the crew raised *Viking*'s mast again, the rigging set, the tent pitched in its place amidships. As they set out, the wind was fresh and the waves choppy, and soon the crew was nearly as wet as they had been crossing the Atlantic.

This was nothing to the experienced crew, but the American students were still with them, and suffered from the wet and the ship's bobbing motion, growing pale and dizzy, and making "sacrifices to the waves" over the side.

With the wind against them, a tugboat towed them to Cleveland, making 11 or 12 miles per hour. At that city, there were more excited spectators, more dignitaries to meet, and more speeches. It was now July 4th.

This time the celebratory flotilla of pleasure boats was decked out in red, white, and blue. The festivities in town included carriage rides, and a festive breakfast. Cleveland was decorated for the holiday, and made a good impression on the Vikings.

They started out late that evening with a contrary wind and choppy water, towed by another tugboat. The next stop would be Detroit, some 87 miles away by water, eight hours by a modern freighter. *Viking* would sail through the night. From

Detroit, they would travel up the Detroit River to Lake Huron, then cross over into Lake Michigan, and sail south to Chicago.

By morning, the wind changed and the waves died down and *Viking*'s movement became more controlled. This water was not like the canal, narrow, constrained, shallow. The Great Lakes were much more like the mighty ocean. *Viking* did not want to poke along behind a coal-driven tugboat. She wanted to play.

Her crew were also anxious to let the Americans see what she could do.

They hoisted the sails, and the towrope began to slacken. Within minutes, they were obviously gaining on the tug. There was not even time to untie the towrope. The rope was cut, and *Viking* sailed past her escort like a racehorse passing a cow.

Gokstad had an estimated top speed of 12 miles an hour. Viking hit 14 that day, and held her pace the rest of the way to Detroit.

The waterway to Detroit was narrow, and both sides, American and Canadian, were thick with spectators. *Viking* was wearing her dragon head and tail, and showing off both her striped mainsail and the striped jib that Rasmussen had made before reaching New York. Her crew fairly burst with pride as they sailed along.

They spent a couple of days in Detroit, waiting for the steamship which would tow *Viking* on the long journey through Lake Huron and down Lake Michigan to Chicago.

The *Albany* was probably one of the "package and passenger freighters" which carried passengers to resorts all through the Great Lakes region. Such ships were both large and fast, and some were described as "floating palaces" or "palace steamers." Rasmussen described her as being the largest steamship he had ever seen.

Viking was hitched up and the journey began. Although she was a fast ship, she was a sailing ship, and needed a good consistent wind to keep a steady speed. Such a wind would probably not be available throughout her trip, so the mechanized ship would tow her, in order to get to Milwaukee on schedule.

Towing at high speed can be a strain on the towed ship. When traveling in this manner, *Viking* lost the advantage of her flexibility, which let her meld with the water when traveling on her own. Rasmussen noticed that her bow was rising a foot higher out of the water than usual, due to the force on the towrope. Still things were perfectly all right for a while.

By evening, the water had turned choppy and the wind was contrary. To a big steamship, this had little effect, but *Viking* was back in a large body of water, where she was relatively small. The rough water and high speed caused her to bounce, and to kick up spray. *Viking*'s crew tried repeatedly to signal *Albion* to slow down. Unfortunately, the larger vessel either took no notice, or did not understand what *Viking* needed. In the many, many signals commonly used for communication between ships, "Slow down, you are towing us too fast!" is *not* one of them.

Spray, and later rain, meant the crew had to bail. It was hard work, and it went on for hours. Everything in the boat was wet. Spray was lifting up, rain was falling down, and even the area under the tent was soaked.

The Norwegians kept at it stoically, but one of the American students finally simply stopped bailing and told the others "I am just not able to get all of Lake Heron out of this boat!"

Finally, finally, Viking raised a pennant meaning "Seek harbor," and *Albion* understood, slowed down and turned toward land. They harbored in Old Mackinaw City. *Albion* had a regular rout through the Great Lakes, and telegrammed her owner, asking "Should we proceed or stay with *Viking*?" The reply was "Stay with *Viking* even if it should take a week."

Another person had been impressed with *Viking* as well. Captain Mikkelsen from Chicago had been onboard during the buffeting she had gotten in the hands of *Albion*. "It's a wonder she wasn't broken into stove-wood by that trip" he said, and then added the saying that had followed *Viking* for thousands of miles "Those old Norsemen certainly knew how to build ships!"

They waited only for the weather to clear – just abut the same time it took for the crew to dry out – and were on their way again at 4:00 pm. At 7:00 pm they made the transition into Lake Michigan, and by 4:00 am of Sunday morning, they were almost in Milwaukee. Just outside the port, a navy ship came to meet them with orders to drop anchor just inside the port's breakwater. This provided shelter from the violent thunderstorm with hail that let loose almost immediately. It was over shortly, however, and soon pleasure boats were coming out to see them.

The American students left them here, vowing to see them in the White City, as the Chicago Exhibition was already being called. Of course, the young men promised never to forget *Viking*, or her crew, or the time they had spent together.

The Welcoming Committee in Milwaukee had invited literally every Norwegian in the state. The Committee came out on a steamer to meet *Viking* on Monday morning, along with another boat, the aptly named *Welcome*, draped in flags and carrying a brass band. The Governor of Wisconsin was there. At 11:00 Viking joined a parade of boats into the Milwaukee River, sailing under her own power, dragon head and tail glinting in the sun. When they reached the middle of town, the sails came down and the men began to row. This had been timed to coincide with the lunch breaks of the city's workforce. Thousands poured out into the Riverwalk to see *Viking*.

A report on the speeches that followed included the following:

> "...at the present time, it is possible to make the journeys that the sagas tell us Leif Erikson had made. By completing his intention, Captain Andersen not only brought Leif Erikson's and the ancient Norseman's discovery of America to be completely acknowledged, but he also captured a place for himself in history..."

Finally, it was acknowledged that, while it might have been impossible for most European ships to do more than creep around the coastlines, the Norse had technologically superior ships which could have, in fact, allowed them to make journeys of discovery a thousand years ago.

All this is perhaps more interesting because the replica *Nina, Pinta* and *Santa Maria* had been in port only a week before. Crowds for *Viking* were estimated at four times the size of the visitors to the more famous trio.

Next day they cleaned the ship, in private, and then went on to Racine. The city greeted them with what was by now customary splendor, and one of the speeches given included:

> This year we celebrate the memory of Christopher Columbus' discovery of America at the great World Exposition in Chicago. This is as it should be, but I still want to remind my listeners

about the irrefutably proven fact that the Norwegians here were the first to discover the country.

Others made friendly jabs at the 3 Spanish ships, pointing out that they had needed to be towed the whole way "Probably to keep them from wandering off..."

The banqueting went on until the middle of the night, and the next day they were on to the Illinois town of Evanston.

USS Michigan – Wikimedia Commons

This was the embarkation point for *Viking*'s grand entrance into the White City. Here they met the USS Michigan, America's first iron-hulled steamer warship. She had three tall sailing masts, as well as a side paddlewheel, and was painted a brilliant white.

Viking was towed by the Revenue Cutter *Andrew Johnson*, a wooden side-wheeler, followed by the Michigan and 32 other navy ships, and then by as many private craft as wanted to come along.

USRC Andrew Johnson - Wikimedia Commons

All the ships were decorated in flags and banners, and all used their steamship whistles to salute Viking with an ear-splitting chorus. All for the little Norwegian ship who had so bravely crossed the Atlantic alone.

At Lincoln Park, the Vikings went onto the *SS Ivanhoe* for lunch and more speeches. Chicago's Mayor, Carter Henry Harrison Sr. came aboard to ceremonially "take control" of *Viking* as a publicity stunt, though only for a short time and always with Captain Andersen standing right at his side. The little ship was sailing under her own power, US and Norwegian flags proudly displayed, dragon head and tail in place. People crowded the shore as even *Viking* had never seen before.

At the Lake Michigan landing place for the Exposition, *Viking* tied up and the Mayor and Captain Anderson mounted a grandstand.

The Mayor spoke to the Vikings and the crowd. He reminded everyone that, while Columbus had done a little discovering, the Norwegians had come to settle in America, all throughout the Midwest, and become good neighbors and friends.

He praised these Vikings, who, unlike their warlike ancestors, had come peacefully, and hoped that relations between Norway and America would always be so friendly. He also, dryly, praised his own city for being a far friendlier place than the "corrupt eastern towns" and promised that the policemen in Chicago were not to be feared.

Then it was time for *Viking* to proceed to Jackson Park, inside the Exposition, her final destination. Here Captain Andersen took off his hat and addressed the crowd. He accepted the praise being heaped upon his men, and lauded them for their hard work and bravery. But he laid the success of their mission on *Viking* herself. Many other Norwegian sailors were brave and hardworking, but there was only one *Viking*. Throughout the voyage, he had known that the sailors would look out for themselves, but the care of this very special ship had been his own, and he had lived in fear that something would happen to her. Now he could put that responsibility down. *Viking* had made it.

Viking at the Great Chicago Columbian Exposition, 1893 – Wikimedia Commons

THE WHITE ⟨ITY, AN⟩ AFTER

The World's Columbian Exposition was a short-lived thing. It began on May 1, 1893, and lasted through the end of October. Forty-six countries attended, and 27 million people bought tickets to see the wonders of the modern world during its six-month run.

Viking had arrived in July, to throngs of cheering thousands. But the journey was the thing, not the destination. Moored, she never attracted the enthusiasm that she had commanded while under sail. It is likely that over a million people saw her on display. But there were other things to see – The amazing traveling walkway, the entire building dedicated to the production and use of electricity, paintings from France, Japan's island of tranquility.

The crew was happy to rest. There were still parties in their honor, but these were private parties and dinners given by private people. (Although usually very rich ones.)

One of the last public actions of the Vikings, as a group, was to gather in the Women's Arts Building, where there was a statue of Leif Erikson. The men joined hands and bowed their heads in a moment of silent communion with their spiritual ancestor.

Statue of Leif Erikson, courtesy of Wikimedia Commons

Eight days after mooring *Viking* in Lincoln Park, the crew was paid off. They had signed on for the trip as crew, not volunteers, with an expecrted payout of 75 Kroner (more for the captain and first mate) with a bonus of 100 Kroner if the captain chose to bestow it. Everyone got the bonus, which they considered quite a handssome payout, though time, distance and culture makes it nearly impossible to equate this to modern American dollars.

Each man was free to go his own way. Some went home, some visited American relatives, some stayed to see the Fair.

Rasmussen continued his own quest, raising funds for a Retired Sailors home in Norway. This had been one of the original goals of the expediton, but the Committee was 12,000 Kroner in debt from *Viking*'s many expenses.

This was the foundation of the problem – What to do with *Viking*? The US Navy wanted her as a gift, and promised generous funds for her upkeep – until it came right down to appropriating money, at which point it became evident that all of the US Navy was not of the same opinion.

Captain Andersen supposedly had Power of Attorney to dispose of his beloved ship as he saw fit, but the Committee was still trying to break even, and the Americans were cheep, so *Viking* did not go to the Navy, or the Smithsonian. It also seems there were many misunderstandings along the way.

As the Fair was breaking up, Captian Andersen realized that *Viking* had the opportunity to go on yet another historic voyage – this time, down the Chicago River, through the Illinois canals to the Mississippi, and down the Mississippi to New Orleans. She would winter in the mild weather of Lousianna, while Andersen returned to Norway. In the spring he would return, and take *Viking* throught the Gulf of Mexico, around Florida, and up the east coast, to Washington DC, where she would be presented to the Smithsonian.

Christensen was with him. They arranged to sail north, away from Jackson Park and into Chicago River on October 31, 1893. Olaf Likerstol, H.H. Hoder, Holwar Larson and Alfred Holm joined them.

At Bridgeport the Chicago River's south branch joined the Illinois & Michigan Canal. It was in a dilapidated state, with crumbling sides and dirty water.

If the Erie Canal had provided some tight places, the Chicago lock system was much worse. Sometimes *Viking* cleared the lock's sides by mere inches, and mattresses had to be used to keep her from damaging herself on the sides. The water was thick, and smelled of sewage.

The trip down the Mississippi was also challenging. Captain Andersen wanted to be quick, because the water was historically low, only four feet deep in places. *Viking* had an eighteen inch keel, and rode a further two feet deep in the water, so she needed a minimum of three and a half feet of water to sail. By now, Andersen knew his ship, though, and carful piloting got her through.

And once she was under sail again, the crowds came back. When *Viking* docked, policemen had to be called out to control the crowds. Andersen, who had always been determined that *Viking*'s voyages not be seen as a comercial venture, was forced to charge for people to get on the ship, simply as a matter of crowd control. At ten cents for adults however, and five cents for children, it did very little to cover expenses, even at 1893 prices.

Once in New Orleans, *Viking* was safely docked. She was in good shape for her upcoming journey to Washington, with most of the equipment she would need already in place. Captain Andersen would go home to Norway for the winter, and then return to take over caring for Viking in the spring.

Except that he never came back. Was it due to meney troubles, family issues, or Andersen's health? History did not record why.

In the spring, *Viking* needed a home. Two Chicago society matrons, Mrs. S. T. Gundersen and Mrs. O. A. Thorp, wanted *Viking* back I n Chicago. She was part of the historic Exposition. The high point, so far, in Chicago's histroy, and they wanted the Exposition memorialized. Already, the Field Columbian Museum was collecting artifacts.

The Museum was housed in the building which had been the Palace of Fine Arts during the Exposition. Most of the buildings, impressive as they were, had been made only for show, constructed like stage sets, never meant to last beyond the six months of the event. Only the Palace of Fine Arts, built to house priceless, borrowed artworks, had been built to last.

The ladies formed a committee, raised funds, and arranged to bring *Viking* back the way she had come.

Upon her return, she was sailed to Lincoln Park again, and put on display in the harbor there. Next were short trips to Racine and Milwaukee, Wisconsin. She returned to Chicago on September 5th, and., while moored, was caught out in a heavy thnderstorm, and filled with water until she was swamped. This was one of the many reasons why she had never been left alone while in the care of the Vikings.

The fireboat *Yosemite* came the next day and pumped until she was up and mostly dry. But she was still a sorry sight, filthy from all the muddly water in her.

First mate Christensen had taken an inventory of all the objects and equipment in *Viking* before turning her over. The list included side lanterns, top lantern, compass, galley equipment and glasses marked "Viking," totally some 200 objects in all. All of this was preserved and turned over to the Field Columbian Museum on October 13, 1984, along with the three Spanish ships built for the Exhibition.

The fledgling museum did not take the preservation of *Viking* seriously. She was put into dry dock on a side porch of the building, not protected from either the elements or the population.

It did not take long for the equipment to begin to disappear. Then people began to take splinters of wood home as souveniers. Day by day, month by month, *Viking* looked worse and worse.

The board was not any better at caring for its facilities, and soon was asking for money for a new building. Their requests did not, however, include space for *Viking*. When the collection moved, in 1920, she remained on the porch of the "old museum," alone.

But the Norwegian community had not forgotten. In 1919, they had begun to raise money to care for her. With the help of the Federation of Norwegian Women's Societies, *Viking* was repaired and installed in an open, roofed structure in Lincoln Park. Officially, ownership was given over to the perpetual care of Commissioners of Lincoln Park. Another banquet was held for *Viking* and the completion of "this notable work."

In 1934, Lincoln Park was consolidated into the Chicago Park District. Though "continued care" for *Viking* was stipulated in the contract, none was evident. Temperatures in Chicago can easily swing by 100 degrees farenheit in the course of a year, and that, and the humidity, did her no good.

She was examined in 1991, and the report found her exterier wood to be in good shape, but her interior degrading, in part because of a coating of bird dropping which, in places, were four inches deep.

The examination also found logs, tools, empty cans and other debris in and around "the object." The report strongly recommended enclosing "the object" and protecting it from the park maintenance crew.

FRIENDS

Archie Andersen, Chairman of the Norwegian National League's Viking Ship Restoration Committee began the ship's restoration, starting by removing all the bird poo.

Sixteen missing sheilds were also replaced, and all the sheilds painted. The head and tail were removed, repainted, and breifly displayed at Navy Pier before being stored at the Museum of Science and Industry. Plans were made for a glass-enclosed home for *Viking*, and money was raised, but a site was never sucured or any other action taken.

In 1993, Lincoln Park made plans to expand, and notified the Viking Ship Restoration Committee that Viking must be moved, or they would consider deeding her to another organizarion. One of the organizations that showed interest was the Vesterheim Norwegian American Museum. The American Scandinavian Council was also interested in her, and wanted to put her in a museum in Chicago.

In 1994, ownership was trandferred from the Chicago Park District to the American Scandinavian Council for the sum of one dollar. The sale stipulated that the Council care for *Viking* and display her in Chicago. In the case that this was not done, ownership would revert to the Park District.

The first thing needed was to hire a professional moving company to build a supportive cradle under *Viking*, and move her and house her temporarily. The Belding Company did the job, housng her in their indoor facility in West Chicago (a suburb 38 miles from Chicago) Belding built a metal support structure, but they were not conversant in the needs of hundred-year-old viking ships. The metal frame they created to stabilize her was not adequate for her needs.

Still, she was out of the weather, at least until Belding was sold in 1996, and the new owner insisted that she be moved. *Viking* was transported to Geneva Illinois and placed in Good Templar Park, under a nylon tent, in 1996.

Officially, The American Scandianvian Council dissolved as a corporation in 2001, and ownership of *Viking* reverted to the Chicago Park District, but they made no move to claim her.

Viking still rested in her metal trasmnporation cradle, but it was not adequate. She began to twist and warp.

Tour groups came to see her,but she was still a sad sight. No longer straight, her deck boards lying in a pile by her side, she occasionally held puddles of water when the cover of the tent blew off.

In 2006, a local news station WTTW, did a segment on *Viking*.

Also in 2006, *Viking* was nominated as one of Illinois' ten most endangered historic sites. In 2007 she made the list. This announcement brought several groups together, and they realized that they would do more good working in unity. The Friends of the Viking Ship was born. Before it could be incorporated, Elizabeth Safanda (a member-to-be) learned about $1,000,000 in grant money beng made available by American Express and The National Trust for Historic Preservation for projects deemed "worthy" via votes in an on-line competitin. She submitted an application for a grant of $52,000 to stabilize the sagging ship.

Twenty-five different projects in the Chicago area were vyiang for the money. Loraine Straw of the Norwegian National League created the website www.vikingship.us to encourage voting, and votes came in from all over the world. In the end *Viking* was awarded the full $52,000 for her preservation.

Meanwhile, Preservation Partners of the Fox Valley and the Norwegian National League partnered with other friends to fund another professional assessment of *Viking*'s condition.

Marine conservator Howard Well examined *Viking* in 2007. Could she be saved? Well provided a 27 page report and an eighteen minute video detailing step to care for *Viking*. He agreed with other examiners – what *Viking* really needed was a climate-controlled home.

Midwest Groundcovers, who had been helping *Viking* for years, improved her tent by replacing it's cover, making it 8 feet longer, and enclosng the ends. Venting was left open, and a door was installed on the end nearest her bow.

Robert Fink went all the way back to the blueprints of *Gokstaad* in order to design proper supports for her daughter, *Viking*. Methods and Material fabricated five side supports, rather than two, additional supports were created for *Viking*'s keel. Wire cables with turnbuckles were added to support the sagging, twisting hull, and the stern post, once the base of the dragon's mighty tail, was brought back to true from an 11 degree bend.

Friends of the Viking Ship NFP was incorporated in 2007. Its sole mission was to care for *Viking* and display her properly. The shelter was improved, a wooden viewing platform was added, so that children could see her better.

In 2008, eight educational posters were added to the display. The Viking Ship Restoration Committee disolved, and transferred all its funds to *Viking*'s Friends. The maintneance committee set up a schedulal of annual cleaning and inspections.

In 2011, her deck boards were washed, measured numbered and photographed. Protective boxes were built to hold and display them.

In 2012, ownership of *Viking* was officially transferred from the Chicago Park District to FOVS. The Friends have already done amazing work preserving *Viking*, and have collected items relevent to her past, including the Raven banner she origianly wore, given by Captain Andersen to the grandfather of Ann Whittier, who came to see Viking in 2011. The FOVS is looking for other items that were original to *Viking* or were made to commemorate her at the World's Exposition.

And the Friends still need help. In spite of many volunteer hours, innovative fund raising, and hundreds of hours of just pain hard work, *Viking* in still in danger. She badly needs a permanent climate controlled space, but space and buildings are expensive, and her Friends do not want to create a shelter that can not be manitained.

The fight for *Viking*'s life goes on, but now she lives where she can be seen, loved, and celbrated, just as she was meant to be.

HOW YOU CAN HELP

Thought *Viking* is finally among friends, she still needs help! Finding a permanent, climate controlled home will take, not only a large initial outlay of money, but ongoing support.

You can help save *Viking*! Go to www.vikingship.us and pledge to donate to her cause. Donations are tax deductable, and after contributing, you can say that you, too, are a part of Viking history.

A portion of the proceeds of this book go to support The Friends of the Viking Ship.

BIBLIOGRAPHY

This book is largely made possible by R. E. Rasmussen's book, <u>Viking: From Norway to America</u>, his personal account as bosun of *Viking* on her journey to the Columbian World's Exposition. The book was originally written in Norwegian, and published in Norway in 1894. It was translated into English by Helen Fletre. The current edition was published by American Solutions for Business, and is only available through the Friends of the Viking Ship.

My initail interest in the Chicago World's Fair was a direct result of reading <u>Devil in the White City</u> by Eric Larson. His passion for the event and immersion in the atmosphere around it will stay with me always.

<u>Wikipedia</u> and <u>Wikimedia Commons</u> may not be considered a really first-rate source for in-depth information, but it's a great place to check dates, get old photos, and scrounge up a little dirt out of someone's back story.

The New York Times' <u>Wayback Machine</u> allowed me to read newspaper articles from over 120 years ago, and really enjoy all the horrible things said about Judge Tighe in response for his attack on the "sturdy Norsemen."

"The Little Scandanavian .com" taught me about *Gokstad*, and I didn't even have to transl;ate it out of Norwegian.

Regia.org's excellent article on "Building a Viking Ship" only increased my enthusiasm for this project. A real passion for the subject matter, here.

Vikingship.us, the official website of the Friends of the Viking Ship was a central point.

And lastly, *Viking* herself, and the wonderful docents who introduced me to her in Good Templar Park one Midsummer day.

Made in the USA
Columbia, SC
24 February 2020